A Library Timeline

ca. 2600 BCE

Royal scribes in Sumer keep records on clay tablets and store them in specially built rooms: the first government libraries.

290 BCE

Pharaoh Ptolemy I builds a great library at Alexandria, Egypt. He wants it to have a copy of every important book in the world.

ca. 1440–1650

The invention of printing makes books quicker, cheaper, and easier to produce.

ca. 100 BCE–300 CE

Rome has big government libraries, and little libraries attached to public baths.

ca. 350 BCE

Wealthy Greeks begin to collect books. They create the first private libraries.

ca. 1500–1800

Wealthy people create great-book collections and give them to universities or governments—the first national libraries.

1858

First horse-and-cart mobile public library brings books to remote communities in England's Lake District. Soon, mobile libraries operate in the United States and many other lands.

2009

The Little Free Library organization begins in the United States. It encourages readers to exchange books at small, friendly volunteer libraries.

1833

The first tax-supported public library opens in the United States. Today, there are thousands of free public libraries worldwide.

ca. 1960s

The first computerized catalogs allow librarians to list books and allow readers to find them.

A Library for Everyone

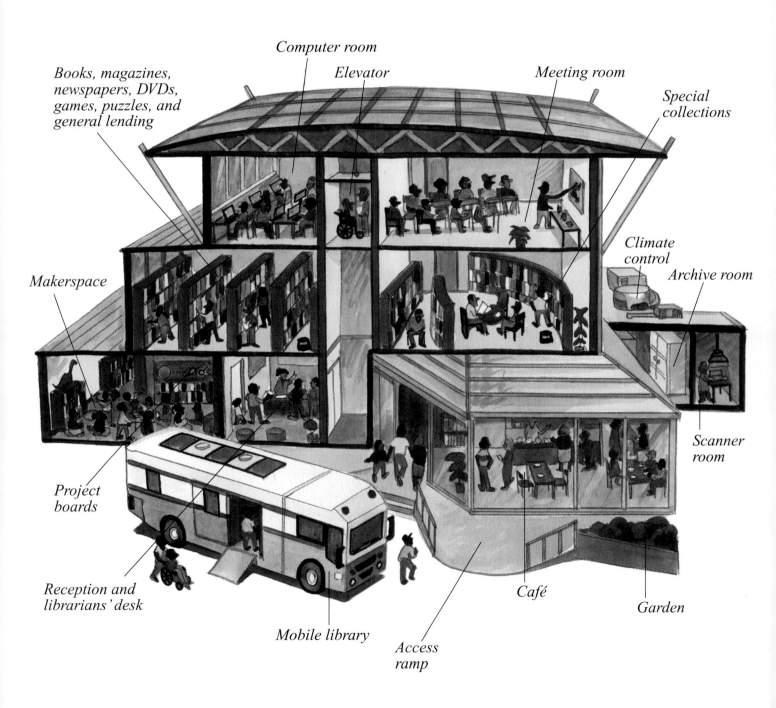

Computer room

Elevator

Meeting room

Books, magazines,
newspapers, DVDs,
games, puzzles, and
general lending

Special
collections

Climate
control

Archive room

Makerspace

Scanner
room

Project
boards

Reception and
librarians' desk

Café

Garden

Mobile library

Access
ramp

Author:

Fiona Macdonald studied history at Cambridge University and at the University of East Anglia, both in England. She has taught adult education, and in schools and universities, and is the author of numerous books for children on historical topics.

Artist:

Mark Bergin was born in Hastings, England, in 1961. He studied at Eastbourne College of Art and specializes in historical reconstructions, aviation, and maritime subjects. He lives in Bexhill-on-Sea with his wife and children.

Editor: Jonathan Ingoldby

Editorial Assistant: Mark Williams

PAPER FROM SUSTAINABLE FORESTS

Published in Great Britain in 2019 by
The Salariya Book Company Ltd
25 Marlborough Place, Brighton BN1 1UB

ISBN-13: 978-0-531-12811-4 (lib. bdg.) 978-0-531-19358-7 (pbk.)

All rights reserved.
Published in 2019 in the United States
by Franklin Watts
An imprint of Scholastic Inc.

A CIP catalog record for this book is available from the Library of Congress.

Printed and bound in China.
Printed on paper from sustainable sources.
1 2 3 4 5 6 7 8 9 10 R 28 27 26 25 24 23 22 21 20 19

SCHOLASTIC, FRANKLIN WATTS, and associated logos are trademarks and/or registered trademarks of Scholastic Inc.

Scholastic Inc., 557 Broadway, New York, NY 10012

You Wouldn't Want to Live Without™
Libraries!

Written by
Fiona Macdonald

Illustrated by
Mark Bergin

Franklin Watts®
An Imprint of Scholastic Inc.

Contents

Introduction

Try, if you can, to imagine a world where books, letters, tweets, texts, and every other kind of writing have disappeared. What would life be like? Would it be simpler, easier—or impossible? Without safe, well-organized collections of written words, how could we check facts or find important information? How would we share stories, beliefs, ideas, and discoveries, or record what we have done?

For 5,000 years and more, libraries have been gathering and preserving writings of all kinds. They're keepers of the world's memory. They're storehouses of knowledge, and imagination, and fun. We wouldn't want to live without them!

Find It Out, Look It Up!

Do you have a library in your school? Do you go to your neighborhood library? If so, you know how important libraries can be. All over the world, millions of people rely on them. Libraries help everyone, from babies who love picture books, to students, scientists, politicians, business people, and many others in search of information. Libraries also offer us poems and stories to read just for fun. They teach us how to find things out, encourage us to think, and help us to learn. Today, we take libraries for granted. But we're very lucky to have them. They weren't always there . . .

A WORLD OF WONDERS.
Library websites bring words and
pictures from all over the world
to our own personal computers.

Top Tip

If you don't yet belong to
your neighborhood library,
ask an adult to help you find
out whether you can join.

Moby Dick,
Chapter 3

MEETING A NEED. Do you
love stories, but can't see to read?
Do you like cooking healthy,
tasty meals but need a cookbook?
Your library can help by loaning
you talking books, and e-books
from its digital collection to read
on your computer.

MULTIMEDIA. Libraries store,
and lend, writings in many different
formats, from old-style books and
papers to the latest digital technology.
Today, a library can be anywhere,
even in your pocket! Modern
communication methods mean we
can link up with libraries whenever
we need to and wherever we go.

It's a Record!

Today, there are libraries all over the world. But when, why, and how did they begin? The first libraries were created to store useful knowledge, such as lists of laws. They were built around 2600 BCE for rulers in Sumer (now in Iraq), where royal scribes kept records of government business, scientific discoveries, myths, and legends. The greatest ancient library was founded by Pharaoh Ptolemy I in 290 BCE at Alexandria, Egypt, to collect all the best books ever written. But these early libraries were not open to everyone. Admittance was by royal invitation only.

A LASTING RECORD. Scribes in Sumer used pens made from reed stalks to scratch picture writing on clay tablets. The records they created have lasted almost 5,000 years.

A new law! Write it down!

Writings from the ancient world have survived because scribes made copies for libraries. If you have important documents, learn from the past, and keep a copy!

EGYPTIANS carved royal records on stone, using hieroglyphs (picture writing), or wrote them in hieratic (flowing script) on sheets of papyrus. But elsewhere . . .

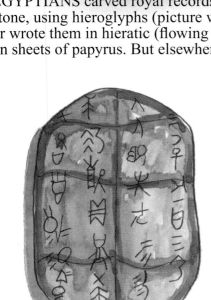

CHINESE scholars inscribed (scratched) lists of names and dates on flat slabs of bone . . .

INCAS IN SOUTH AMERICA kept their records in mathematical code by making patterns of knots in string quipus . . .

IN AFRICA, some of the world's very first records were carved on stone and stored in caves . . .

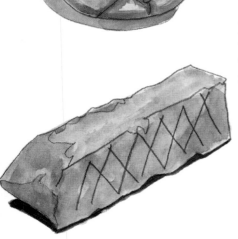

SCRIBES IN MUSLIM LANDS wrote in beautiful writing on pages of parchment, then bound them together to create books.

Our Books, Our History, Ourselves

Early libraries preserved beliefs and ideas. Everywhere written records were kept, libraries were valued as guardians of national culture, history, and identity. It's the same today. National libraries keep a copy of every book published in their home country. Presidential libraries keep US presidents' papers, records, and other historical documents. It would be a disaster if this heritage—which belongs to all of us—were lost or destroyed. Libraries also keep collections of local books, photos, and documents about neighborhoods and communities. We need these. We need libraries!

LEADER OF LEARNING. In 1814, former US president Thomas Jefferson handed over his collection of 6,487 books to the new national Library of Congress (founded in 1800).

So much to research today!

NATIONAL TREASURES. We trust libraries to store precious historical documents. The Magna Carta, written in 1215, is kept in the British Library in London (founded in 1753).

You Can Do It!

Make a memory archive. Fill a scrapbook or a shoebox with letters, poems, and pictures that are important to you and your life story.

INTERNATIONAL KNOWLEDGE. Libraries set up over 1,000 years ago by Middle Eastern Muslim rulers collected rare, ancient, scientific writings and saved them for future generations.

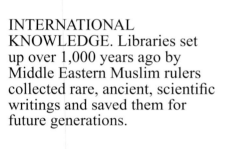

TODAY'S NEWS, TOMORROW'S HISTORY. Libraries also collect information about important events today, from sports championships and space exploration to campaigns for civil rights.

OUR OWN STORY. Library archives of letters, diaries, newspapers, photos, and memories recorded by older people keep the history of our communities alive.

Print and Progress

Today, we are fortunate. Books are relatively inexpensive and most communities have libraries. However, for thousands of years, written records were rare and very valuable. It took a year for a scribe to make just one copy of a book—slowly, by hand. The finished volume was then locked away. Ordinary people had no chance of reading it. But around 1440, in Germany, there was a technological revolution when the printing press was invented. Printing by machine meant that many copies of a text could be produced, quickly and cheaply. Ordinary people, eager for knowledge and entertainment, began to set up little libraries to share books among themselves.

NEW! PRINTED PAGES! German gold worker Johannes Gutenberg (ca. 1400–1468) arranged metal letters to make words, rubbed them with ink, and pressed paper on top to print copies. The movable-type printing press was born.

OH SO SLOW. Old-style, slowly made, handwritten books were so valuable that they were often chained to shelves for safe-keeping.

Members of subscription libraries paid yearly fees (called subscriptions). The money was used to buy new books for their library.

WINDOW ON THE WORLD. From about 1500 on, printed copies of maps, pictures, and travelers' tales helped spread amazing news of distant peoples and places.

WHAT ABOUT THE WORKERS? Working people were also eager to read. They joined together to buy books, and set up reading rooms where they could study in the evenings and on weekends.

PAY TO READ. If you had money, you could pay to borrow books from a circulating library or join a private reading club, known as a subscription library. The first subscription library in the United States opened in 1731. At first, it was for men only.

READING ROOM

13

Public Libraries: Open to All

Today, most libraries are public libraries. They welcome anyone who wants to use their services, for free. Unlike people in the past, we don't need money or wealthy friends to have access to reading materials. We're so lucky! The first tax-supported public library was opened in 1833, in Peterborough, New Hampshire. Soon after, laws encouraged public libraries throughout Europe and America. Today, public libraries still lend books, but they also provide computers and WiFi, offer expert help and advice, and run study groups, clubs, and online courses. They give everyone the chance to enjoy reading and learning.

FREE AND FANTASTIC. Opened in 1854, Boston Public Library was the first big-city public library in the United States. Since 1895, it has been housed in a splendid building, designed as "a palace for the people."

TEMPLES OF LEARNING. Scottish-American businessman Andrew Carnegie (1835–1919) paid for over 2,500 public libraries in the United States and worldwide.

Who pays for free public libraries today? We all do! Money to run public libraries, including the cost of library cards that help to keep a record of the books you have borrowed and returned, comes from national and local taxes.

LEARN TO LOVE your local public library. Knowledge is power!

MEETING POINT. Many public libraries have cafés or public rooms where readers can meet, talk, and share news and views. This helps build stronger, closer communities. Another great library service!

REACHING OUT. You can find public libraries in big cities and tiny towns. This cool, airy, public library is suited to the hot, local climate.

Lending and Borrowing

There are few nicer things to do on a cold, dark evening than curl up in a comfy chair with a new library book, especially if it's a story by your favorite author. Libraries often keep multiple copies of books by popular writers, so several people can borrow them without having to wait. You can also borrow a digital copy or e-book to read on a computer or mobile device. Mobile libraries lend books to readers in remote areas. Little lending libraries, mostly run by book-loving volunteers, appear in all sorts of places. Borrowing is free, and borrowers often bring their own favorite books to lend and share.

BOOKS ON BOARD. Mobile libraries come in a surprising variety of shapes and sizes!

WELCOME VISITORS.
Can't get to your local library?
In some places, community librarians can loan books to you at home.

You Can Do It!

Make a list of the five books that you would most like to borrow from your school or neighborhood library. Ask a friend to do the same, and then compare your lists.

BOOKS ON THE BEACH.
Bored by sunbathing? Then set up a seaside library. Bring a book of your own, and take another one away.

AFTER HOURS. Need to borrow a book—urgently—but the library is closed? Helpful book-lending machines have been around since 1822, with more success in some countries than others!

GOT SOME SPARE SPACE for books? Then set up a little free library and lend to friends and strangers. Even an old roadside mailbox will do!

17

Special Collections

Are you delighted by dinosaurs? Passionate about pirates? Giddy about graphic novels? Clever at chess? Crazy about clocks or cats or cheese? If so, there's almost certainly a library with a special collection of books, papers, photos, maps, or models that's just what you'd love to see! There are thousands of libraries run by private organizations for readers with special interests, from athletics to zookeeping, music to mechanics, law to rocket science, and much more. Public and private libraries also keep collections for minority groups, political organizations, and government departments—including the armed forces and the secret service.

ALL TOGETHER. University libraries have huge rooms full of computers so that hundreds of students can write papers and study for exams, all at the same time.

Some special libraries can be visited by the public. Others are strictly for members only.

A LIBRARY OF OUR OWN. Political groups, such as those demanding rights for women, often have their own special libraries and picture archives.

SINGLE SUBJECT. Some famous people from the past, like playwright William Shakespeare (1564–1616), have whole libraries devoted to the study of their work.

OUR FAITH, OUR BOOKS. Many places of worship have libraries of books about religion for believers—and their friends—to share.

Librarians

They may speak quietly. They may look calm. But your local librarians are actually supermen and superwomen, full of expert knowledge and highly trained to help you. In addition to issuing books and guiding and advising readers, librarians work with teachers and community groups to develop new services. They run classes and clubs, and find answers to questions of all kinds. They supervise library spaces and train volunteers. They give talks. They write blogs. They buy new books to please patrons, and make sure that collections of photos, films, and documents are carefully preserved. Libraries couldn't survive without librarians!

FACTS AND FIGURES. Librarians have to keep careful records. They track things such as what books are popular, what times the library is busiest, and what new services patrons need.

COMPUTER CONFIDENCE. Need to know how to use the latest information technology? Ask a librarian. They'll help you.

IN OR OUT? Library collections keep changing. Some old books have to go, to make space for new ones. But how to choose? A librarian knows!

Top Tip

Ask your school or neighborhood librarian about services for young library members. You might be surprised at how many there are.

Goodbye, old friend!

STORY TIME. Reading is an essential life skill. So librarians help children learn to love all sorts of books by holding fun storytelling sessions with songs, performances, and even science activities.

FUNDRAISER. Some librarians raise money to improve library services by lobbying government, businesses, and private donors. They may be involved in community fundraising, too.

Sorting, Storing, Security

Do you know how to find the library book you need? Libraries contain hundreds, thousands, maybe millions of volumes. They can't all be mixed up on the shelves together! To organize books, librarians classify (sort) them into groups. (You can read more about this on page 34.) Then they give each book its own barcode and classification number. Library books also have to be stored very safely. Some are priceless! To guard against theft, libraries have hidden cameras, alarms, and security guards. Smoke detectors, heat sensors, fire extinguishers, and water sprinklers protect books from fire.

LONG AGO, ancient Greeks and Romans stored parchment scrolls in big baskets, and gave each scroll a little name tag as a means of identifying it.

Some libraries stop insects from harming their collections by freezing old books and documents before allowing them into a library.

DEEP FREEZE

STORAGE SOLUTION. Bookcases with locking doors were invented around 400 CE. In addition to preventing theft, they helped keep books safe from rats, mice, and insects. These destructive pests can still cause damage in libraries today.

TOO HOT, TOO COLD? Extreme temperatures can ruin books and documents. Modern air-conditioning systems help protect library collections.

LIBRARY LIST. A catalog is a classified list of everything in a library. It lets readers—and librarians—know what's stored on the shelves.

So old-fashioned! Our catalog is computerized!

ROBOTS HELP READERS. In big, modern libraries, book storage is managed by computer-controlled systems such as moving shelves and automatic lifts. Sometimes, robots—not librarians—retrieve books for readers.

HANDS OFF! Germs, oils, and sweat on human hands can harm fragile books and documents. So librarians make digital copies, which can be read online without the originals being touched.

23

A Chance to Learn

There are many ingenious ways in which libraries help people develop new abilities and discover fresh opportunities. Guest speakers can talk about true-life events, and "reading dogs" can befriend nervous readers and make them more relaxed about the library experience. Libraries are about learning, and it's never too late—or too early—to begin. Library learning starts with baby bedtime stories and continues throughout life. Some library classes are just for fun; others help library patrons catch up on missed schooling, work for their communities, or acquire a new skill to help them succeed in their career.

HOMEWORK HELPER. Like thousands of children worldwide, these students have gone to the library to get help with their homework.

ART FOR ALL. Painting, drawing, model-making, pottery . . . you'll probably find at least one art class at a library near you. Library classes are not only a way to learn new skills, they can also be a great way to make new friends.

Top Tip

Find out what classes or clubs are available for young readers at your school or neighborhood library.

SEE WHAT I SAY. Many libraries hold classes for people with disabilities. This teacher is helping deaf students learn sign language.

JOIN THE CLUB. Book clubs meet regularly, often in libraries. Members read new books and discuss them together.

READ THE BOOKS, FEEL THE BEAT! Some libraries hold dance classes for readers. Everyone is encouraged to "bring their dancing shoes."

Book Club

Books and Much, Much More!

Do you bring home only books or DVDs from the library? Or have you ever tried to borrow other items? Some libraries offer an amazing choice, from costumes, sewing machines, and sports equipment, to cameras, telescopes, and trombones. However, not all libraries can afford to have so many different items in their collections. Libraries in the United States are ready to lend the biggest, strangest objects. Elsewhere, the items most usually borrowed are small and easily carried: toys, pictures, sheet music, console games, laptops, and household repair tools. Most are safely returned by borrowers. That's good to know!

Oh my word! What DO you have there?!

We borrowed them from the library!

GET CREATIVE! Love painting? Can't afford expensive equipment? Then look for a library that lends it. That way, you'll have a better chance to develop your artistic skills.

How It Works

Want to read a book, but your library doesn't have it? Ask the librarian to borrow it from another library. This is called an interlibrary loan.

But all the others had been borrowed . . .

WANT TO BAKE A CAKE? Then borrow a pan from a library—but be careful to choose the right size and type!

Stop! That's borrowed! It has to go back!

GREEN THUMB? Borrow seeds from a library, plant them, and watch them grow. When your plants produce ripe seeds, take some back to the library to lend to others.

WHAT A PUZZLE! It's great to test your wits with a nice new jigsaw puzzle from the library. There's only one problem: how to keep all the pieces safe!

A Place in the Community

Which are the most important buildings in your community? Schools? Yes! Hospitals? Yes! Shopping malls? Yes! Sports centers? Yes! And also libraries! The first libraries were just safe storage spaces for government records. But today, they do so much more. Libraries still lend books—of course!—but we also value them as friendly, pleasant places where we can meet and think, discover and have fun. In many ways, libraries help us and our communities to become the best that we can be. We really wouldn't want to live without them.

. . . if we need advice, information, or help with problems . . .

Libraries have something for us all . . .

. . . if we're hunting for new knowledge, or checking facts and figures . . .

. . . if we're very young readers, or very old ones . . .

. . . if we want to learn new skills, and make new friends . . .

You Can Do It!

Find out how you can help your local library. Do they need book donations? Help raising money? Or once you are old enough, you could volunteer there!

. . . or grow more confident, by practicing and playing.

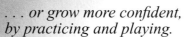

Best of all, books and libraries inspire us. They are a springboard to lifelong pleasure. Anything might be possible, if we read, and think, and dream!

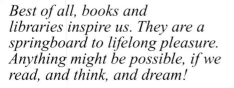

Glossary

Archive Collection of old documents, maps or photos, stored safely because they contain important information or ideas.

Barcode Pattern of black lines and white spaces; a code that computers and other digital machines can read. It is used in libraries to record book-borrowing and by businesses to monitor sales in stores and track package deliveries.

Catalog A well-organized list. A library catalog lists and describes all the items in a library.

Circulating library Type of library run by bookstores from around 1700 to 1950. Readers paid for each book they borrowed.

Classify Arrange in groups. Library books are usually classified by subject matter, or sometimes by the name of the author.

Digital collections Library material stored and loaned in a digital format. This can include e-books and digital copies of old-style books and papers.

Donor Person who gives money or goods to help a good cause.

E-book A digital version of a printed book to be read on a computer, tablet, or other electronic device.

Founded Set up, built, and paid for.

Heritage Objects such as buildings, works of art, and books surviving from the past that are important to the history of a people or a nation.

Hieratic script A type of handwriting, based on hieroglyphs, used by government scribes in ancient Egypt.

Hieroglyphs Picture-writing used mainly for carving on monuments in ancient Egypt.

Inscribed Scratched on a hard surface.

Interlibrary loan When one library borrows a book from another library.

Lobbying Talking to powerful people and decision makers, to try to convince them of your point of view.

Magna Carta (Latin: Great Charter)
A document drawn up in 1215 in England. It is honored today because it says that all government leaders must obey the law.

Multiple copies Many copies of the same book or paper.

Papyrus Material for writing on (an early kind of paper), made in ancient Egypt from the stalks of reeds.

Parchment Cleaned, trimmed skin from sheep or goats, used to write on, between around 500 BCE and 1500 CE.

Pharaoh Title of the kings of ancient Egypt. It comes from words meaning "great house" or "royal palace."

Preserved Cared for, cleaned, and repaired. Libraries with old books and documents have expert conservators who look after library collections to make sure that they stay in good condition.

Quipu Device for recording information, used by the Inca people of South America until around 1550.

Reading room A place where working people met to share books and study together.

Reed A tall, strong plant (a type of grass) that grows in water.

Scribe Person who is skilled at writing, and who makes a living from writing or copying letters, books, and documents.

Subscription library Collection of books paid for and used only by people who paid a yearly fee (subscription) to belong to the library.

Talking books Books read out loud and recorded by actors with clear, pleasant voices.

Index

Top Facts About Libraries

In 2016, over half the adults in the United States and the United Kingdom had a library membership card.

The peak age of people who use the library is between 15 and 25 years. People over 55 are the least likely to visit a library.

In 2015, there were 98,460 school libraries in the United States, and American students made 1.5 billion visits to them. In Britain in the same year, 7 out of every 10 students said they had recently used a library.

Our word *library* originates from the Latin word *liber*, which means "book." The Romans (who spoke Latin) used the same word to mean "bark from a tree," which they sometimes used to write on.

The largest library in the world is the Library of Congress in Washington, D.C. It contains over 167 million items, stored on 838 miles (1,348 kilometers) of shelves. It employs over 3,000 expert staff, and almost half a billion readers consulted its website in 2016.

If you went to the British Library in London and looked at five items a day, it would take you over 80,000 years to see the whole collection of around 150 million items.

In 2016, libraries in the United States spent 2.26 billion dollars on books, information technology, staff, and buildings. That's an amazing investment in learning!

Classification Systems

There are various ways of classifying books in libraries. One of the most widely used systems was invented by Melvil Dewey in the United States in 1873. It is based on subject matter. This means that all the books about the same topic are arranged close together on the shelves.

Have you seen books labeled with these Dewey classifications in your local library?

000 — Computer science, information, and general works
100 — Philosophy and psychology
200 — Religion
300 — Social sciences
400 — Language
500 — Pure science
600 — Technology
700 — Arts and recreation
800 — Literature
900 — History and geography

Alternative classification methods exist, such as the Library of Congress system. Also, many public and school libraries now organize their collections by genre.

Did You Know?

In 1849, a young British explorer named Austen Henry Layard discovered a heap of clay tablets buried under the floor of an ancient toilet. He was astonished to learn that they were 2,500 years old, and came from the great royal library at Nineveh (now in Iraq).

The Great Library at Alexandria in Egypt, founded in 290 BCE, contained over 700,000 books written on scrolls of papyrus. Ships arriving at Alexandria harbor were searched by government officials. Any books found on board were taken away, and given to the library. Sadly, most books in the Alexandria Library were destroyed by attacking invaders and by fires. By 642 CE, the Great Library was in ruins. To the great loss of our civilization, experts estimate that only 2 out of every 10 books from the ancient world have survived.

Ancient Romans liked to read at the baths. Roman public baths were like modern leisure centers, with pools, cafés, gyms, beauty salons—and also libraries. There, readers could learn about history, politics, science, and philosophy, or enjoy the latest poems and plays.

The oldest library still open to readers today was founded in Fez, Morocco, by a merchant's daughter, Fatima al-Fihri, in 859 CE. Fatima also gave money to help build a university and a mosque.

Since ancient Egyptian times, librarians have kept cats to protect books from rats and mice. Today, some libraries also value cats for the calm, relaxed feeling they create for readers.